Simple Machines
Screws

by Martha E. H. Rustad

CAPSTONE PRESS
a capstone imprint

Little Pebble is published by Capstone Press,
1710 Roe Crest Drive, North Mankato, Minnesota 56003
www.mycapstone.com

Library of Congress Cataloging-in-Publication Data
Names: Rustad, Martha E. H. (Martha Elizabeth Hillman), 1975– author.
Title: Screws / by Martha E.H. Rustad.
Description: North Mankato, Minnesota : Capstone Press, 2018. | Series:
    Little pebble. Simple machines | Audience: Ages 4–7.
Identifiers: LCCN 2017031585 (print) | LCCN 2017035878 (ebook) |
    ISBN 9781543500844 (eBook PDF) | ISBN 9781543500721 (hardcover) |
    ISBN 9781543500783 (paperback)
Subjects: LCSH: Screws—Juvenile literature.
Classification: LCC TJ1338 (ebook) | LCC TJ1338 .R87 2018 (print) | DDC
    621.8/82—dc23
LC record available at https://lccn.loc.gov/2017031585

Editorial Credits
Marissa Kirkman, editor; Kyle Grentz (cover) and Charmaine Whitman (interior), designers;
Jo Miller, media researcher; Katy LaVigne, production specialist

Image Credits
Alamy: Ted Foxx, 11; Getty Images: Flashpop, 21; Shutterstock: Adam Gryko, 10, domnitsky,
9, encierro, cover, 1, Georgi Roshkov, 22, goodluz, 5, Grigvovan, 13, Michal Bellan, 7,
Rasstock, 17, RTimages, 14, sirtravelalot, 15, Studio ART, 19, Vadim Ratnikov, 6

Design Elements
Capstone

Printed and bound in the USA.
010766S18

Table of Contents

Help with Work

Work is hard!

We need help.

Use a simple machine.

These tools help us work.

screw

A screw holds things together.

It can lift things too.

screw

Parts

A screw has a post.

The thread goes around it.

See the point.

See the head.

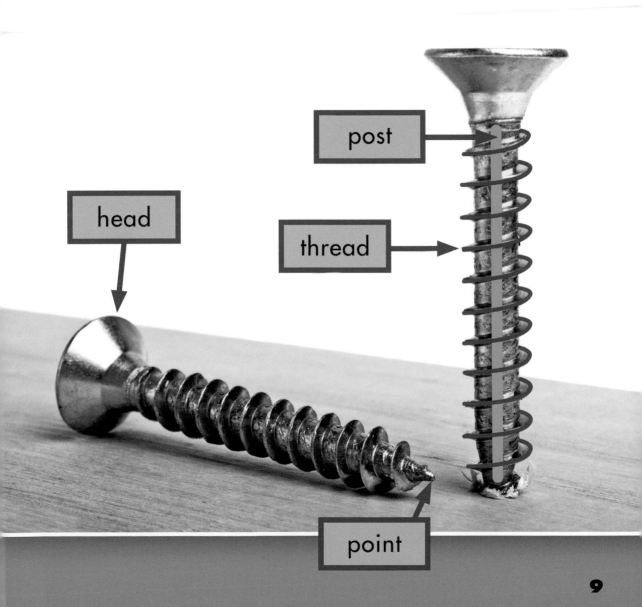

post

head

thread

point

Turn the screw.

It moves up or down.

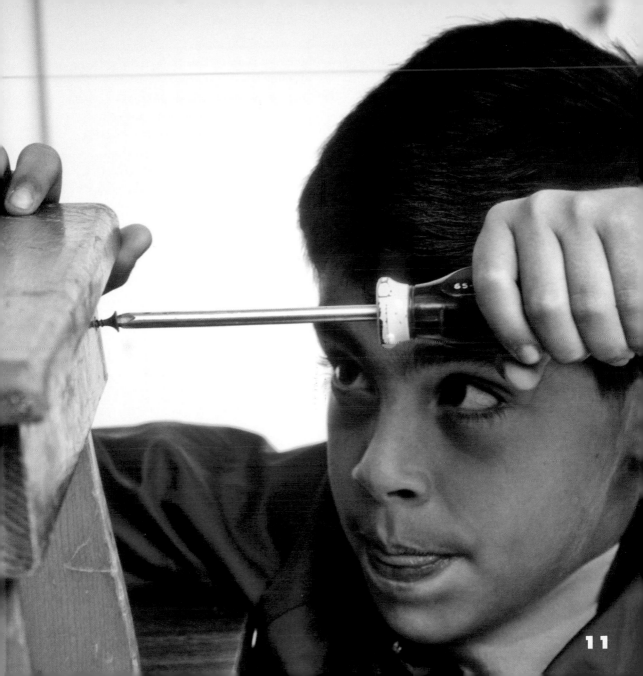

The screw is down.

It holds a load.

The load stays in place.

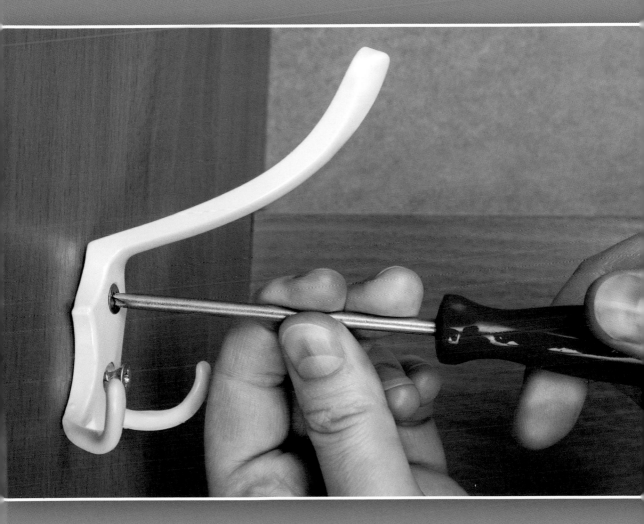

Everyday Tools

A lid is a screw.

Twist!

The jar is open.

14

A light bulb has a screw.

Turn!

The bulb stays in place.

A sink has a screw.

Whoosh!

Water comes out.

We get help from
a simple machine.
It makes work easier and fun.

Glossary

load—an object that you want to move or lift

screw—a simple machine that holds things together

simple machine—a tool that makes it easier to do something

thread—a long thin ridge along a screw

tool—an item used to make work easier

work—a job that must be done

Read More

LaMachia, Dawn. *Screws at Work.* Zoom in on Simple Machines. New York: Enslow Publishing, 2016.

Miller, Tim and Rebecca Sjonger. *Screws in My Makerspace.* Simple Machines in My Makerspace. New York: Crabtree Publishing, 2017.

Schuh, Mari. *Going Ice Fishing: Lever vs. Screw.* Simple Machines to the Rescue. Minneapolis: Lerner Publications, 2016.

Internet Sites

Use FactHound to find Internet sites related to this book.

Visit www.facthound.com

Just type in 9781543500721 and go.

Super-cool stuff!

Check out projects, games and lots more at
www.capstonekids.com

Critical Thinking Questions

1. What happens when you turn the screw?

2. What part of the screw does the thread go around?

3. What objects do you use that have screws in them?

Index